THE BRIGHT SIDE

Finding Strength in Adversity

Sheresse Winford

Struggles to Success
A Series of Hope and Inspiration

A Series of Hope and Inspiration

® Copyright 2024, Sheresse Winford

All rights reserved. No portion of this book may be reproduced by mechanical, photographic, or electronic process, nor may it be stored in a retrieval system, transmitted in any form or otherwise be copied for public or private use without written permission of the copyright owner.

For more information contact:
www.figfactormedia.com

Cover Design and Layout by DG Marco Antonio Álvarez Rodríguez
Printed in the United States of America

ISBN: 978-1-961600-32-4

Library of Congress Control Number: 2024921294

THE BRIGHT SIDE

Finding Strength
in Adversity

Dedication

This book is dedicated to my mother, Carolyn Winford, and also in loving memory of my Father, Jesse Winford.

Table of Contents

6   **Acknowledgments**

8   **Introduction**

11   Chapter 1: **Life's Journey of Growth**

15   Chapter 2: **Building Roots**

19   Chapter 3: **Triumph Through Sacrifice**

23   Chapter 4: **New Horizons, New Challenges**

27   Chapter 5: **Love and Challenges**

31   Chapter 6: **The Power of Community**

35   Chapter 7: **Navigating Family Dynamics with Love**

39   Chapter 8: **Choosing Love Over Conflict**

43   Chapter 9: **Learning from Life's Lessons**

47   Chapter 10: **Embracing Hope in Adversity**

51   Chapter 11: **The Strength of a Mother's Love**

55   Chapter 12: **Finding Peace Through Reflection**

59   Chapter 13: **Inspiration and Hope for the Future**

62   **About the Author**

Acknowledgments

A huge thank you goes out to my beautiful daughter, Roynetta Tripp, for supporting my ideas and always encouraging me to push forward. She is my biggest cheerleader.

Thank you also to Terry Knight for supporting me in everything that I do.

Introduction

The Bright Side: Finding Strength in Adversity is more than just a personal narrative. It's a story of survival, resilience, and hope. In this, the first in a three-book series, Sheresse Winford shares the deeply personal and sometimes painful experiences that shaped her into the person she is today.

Her life has been filled with hardships—battles with addiction, homelessness, loss, and personal struggle, but Sheresse's story is not just about the struggles themselves. It's about the lessons she learned from those challenges and how they fueled her determination to transform her life.

Through each chapter, Sheresse reflects on crucial moments in her life—her father's addiction, her mother's strength, the hardships of growing up in a turbulent environment, and her eventual path to redemption. These events resonate on a universal level, and you are invited to reflect on your life, struggles, and how you, too, can find the strength to overcome adversity.

Sheresse's life took her through an 18-year journey of street life, addiction, and personal destruction, a period she often refers to as her "old life." But it was at her lowest point—imprisoned, addicted, and homeless—that she made a powerful decision to ask for help and change her life.

Through her faith, Sheresse found a way out of the darkness, reaching out to God and ultimately beginning her "new life." This transformation is at the heart of *The Bright Side*. No matter how far someone has fallen or how dark the path has become, there is always a way back to light.

This book is a call to action for those who may be struggling or know someone who is. Sheresse's message is clear: if she can change, anyone can. Her journey proves that we are not defined by our past mistakes but by how we rise from them. Every challenge in life offers a lesson, and every hardship is an opportunity for growth. The experiences we go through, though painful, shape us into stronger, more compassionate individuals.

Throughout the book, Sheresse gently invites us to reflect on our own experiences. Each chapter ends with a reflective question, prompting you to think about your own journey. These questions are not just rhetorical—they are designed to help you actively engage with the content to find your strength and resilience in the face of adversity.

At its core, *The Bright Side* is about transformation. It's about the power of hope, the strength that comes from faith, and the beauty of human resilience. Sheresse's story reminds us that even in our darkest moments, there is always a bright side. We just need to find it.

Sheresse's story is relatable and inspiring, offering hope for those facing their own struggles. Her resilience proves that even in our lowest moments, we are capable of extraordinary growth. By the end of *The Bright Side*, you will not only feel inspired by Sheresse's journey but also empowered to confront your own obstacles with courage.

Chapter 1:

Life's Journey of Growth

Life is not always predictable, and I've realized that the blend of blessings and hardships we face forms the foundation of who we are. Reflecting on my journey, it's clear that each challenge was an opportunity to grow, and each moment of hardship was a teacher in disguise.

At times, I didn't understand why certain things happened. Why did life seem so difficult while others seemed to move forward with ease? But looking back, I see that it was in those hard moments that I found my strength.

I was born into a family of love but also into a family that faced its own battles. My parents had a deep love for one another, but they also encountered struggles that tested their relationship. Through their journey, I learned that love and hardship often coexist.

Those struggles taught me resilience, patience, and the understanding that life, no matter how hard, is full of lessons waiting to be discovered. Every difficult moment we faced helped me learn more about myself and the world around me.

There were days when I wished for easier times and circumstances that didn't feel so heavy. But in time, I came to realize that every storm passes, and when it does, it leaves behind a clearer sky. I grew to understand that the strength I built through those storms was the greatest gift of all.

Life taught me that growth doesn't come from ease—it comes from pushing through the hard times, embracing the lessons along the way, and choosing to see the light even when the world feels dark.

Finding Strength in Adversity

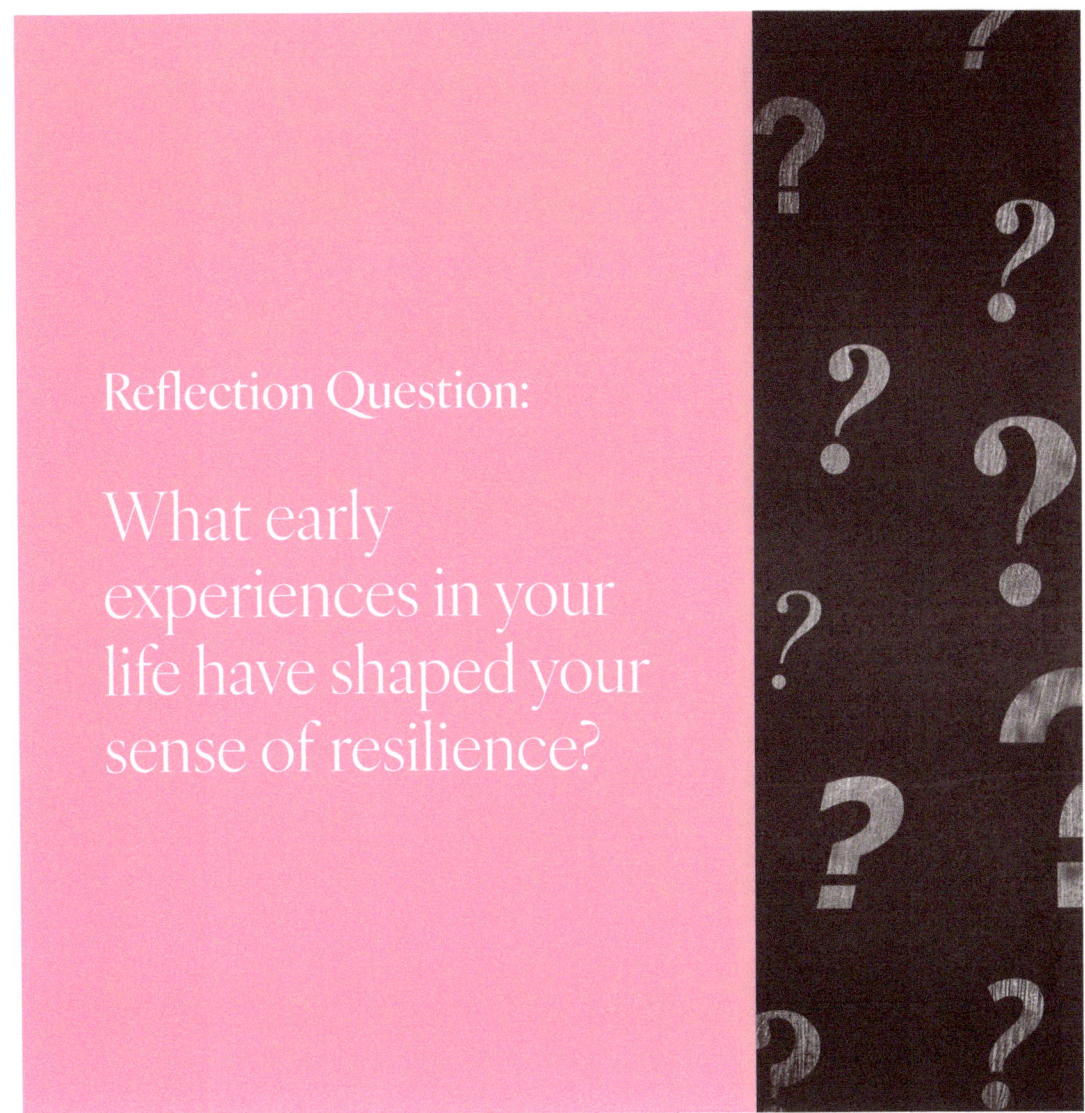

Reflection Question:

What early experiences in your life have shaped your sense of resilience?

Chapter 2:

Building Roots

My parents' love story was complex, filled with moments of joy, hope, and struggle. They met in high school, and from the very beginning, their connection was undeniable. It wasn't a story of easy love but of determination, growth, and perseverance. They came from different backgrounds, yet their shared dreams brought them together, creating a bond that would lay the foundation for our family.

Their relationship was far from perfect, but it was real. My parents faced their fair share of challenges—early parenthood, financial struggles, and the pressure of making ends meet. But they shared a deep commitment to one another and to us, their children.

My mother, determined to finish her education, leaned on the family for support, while my father worked hard to provide all we needed. Together, they created a life for us, and in their sacrifices, they built the roots that allowed our family to grow strong.

I learned early on that love is not without its struggles. The relationships I grew up around were filled with both joy and hardship and through them, I realized that love is not defined by the absence of conflict but by the commitment to working through it.

My parents' love story taught me that the strongest bonds are forged in both good times and bad. They showed me that even when life gets hard, love—rooted in trust and perseverance—can help you weather any storm.

As I look back over their journey, I now understand that the roots they planted in love and resilience became the foundation for my understanding of what it means to love and be loved. Their story is the reason I believe that no matter how difficult life becomes, the relationships we build on trust and dedication will always hold us steady.

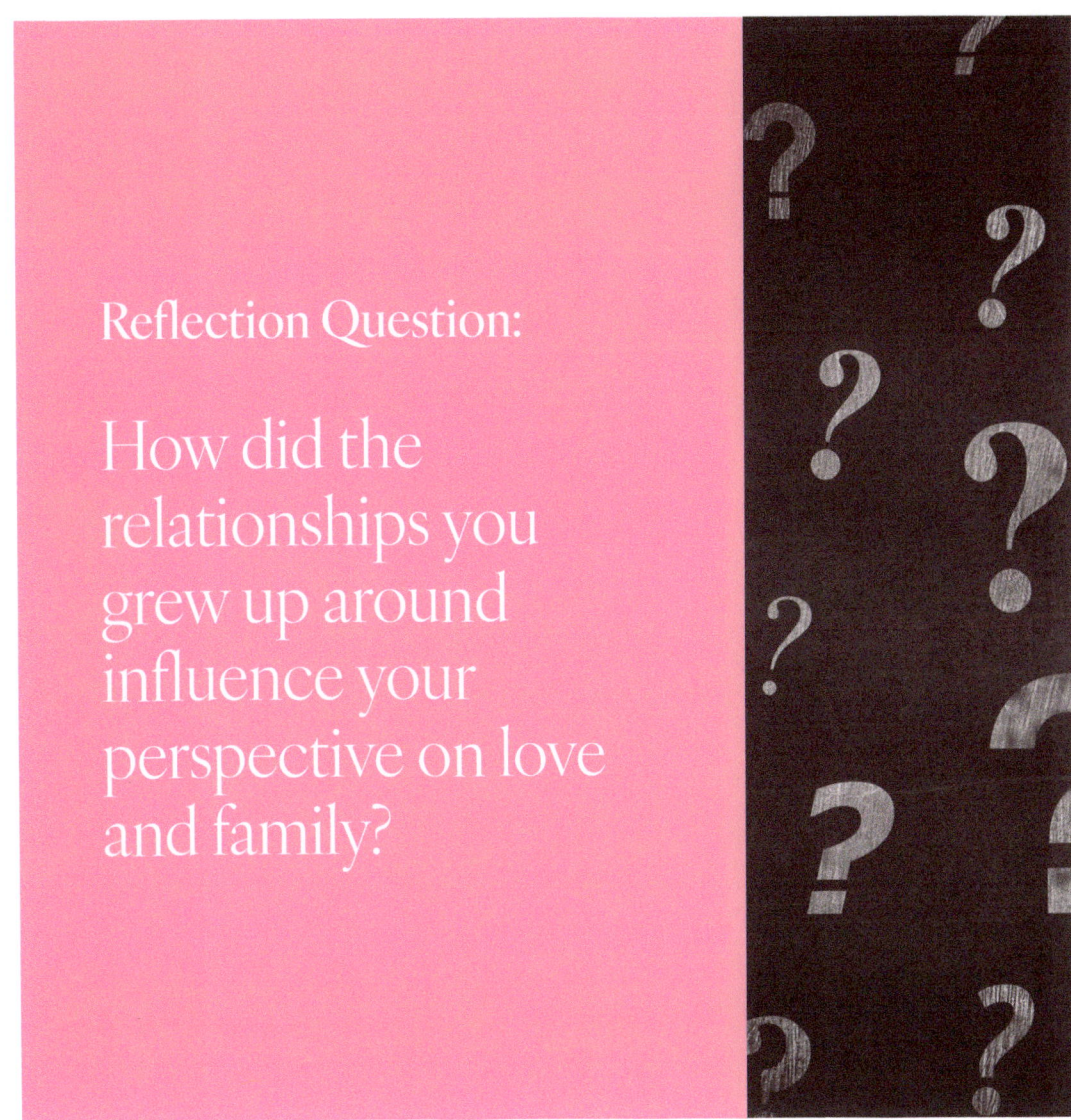

Reflection Question:

How did the relationships you grew up around influence your perspective on love and family?

Chapter 3:

Triumph Through Sacrifice

My mother's strength and resilience shaped my understanding of what true sacrifice looks like. She became a mother as a teenager, facing the challenges of raising my brother while still trying to finish school. It wasn't easy, but she refused to let her circumstances define her future. With the support of her family and her determination to graduate from high school, she decided to continue her education despite the challenges she faced.

Even when my mother was overwhelmed, she never gave up. She balanced motherhood, school, and work with grace, knowing that the sacrifices she made today would create a better tomorrow for us. I often think back on how she managed to hold everything together, working tirelessly to give us a life filled with love and possibilities. She embodied perseverance, and through her journey, I learned that true strength is born in moments of struggle.

Her sacrifices weren't just physical. They were emotional as well. I could see the weight she carried and the dreams she set aside to ensure our needs came first. Yet, she never complained. She gave without expecting anything in return, showing me that love is more than just words—it's action, too. Watching her navigate those difficult years taught me how to handle challenges in my own life, and I've realized that the foundation of any success is built on love, sacrifice, and commitment.

Through her, I learned that the greatest triumphs come from the hardest struggles. Her tenacity and selflessness inspire me to this day. In many ways, her sacrifices became the building blocks of my own strength, teaching me that no act of love, however small or large, is ever in vain. Her journey is the reason I believe in the power of love and perseverance to overcome even the greatest of obstacles.

Finding Strength in Adversity

Reflection Question:

What acts of sacrifice have inspired you in your own life, and how have they shaped your character?

Chapter 4:

New Horizons, New Challenges

When my family made the decision to move to Chicago, it felt like the beginning of something new. The promise of a bigger city held the allure of more opportunities—a chance for us to start over and build the life my parents had always dreamed of.

However, what we didn't realize was that new horizons bring their own set of challenges. Moving to a bustling city wasn't just about fresh starts. It also meant adapting to a different environment and facing new struggles.

At first, the excitement of being in a new place helped us push through the initial hardships. My parents were eager to find work and establish our lives in this unfamiliar environment, but the reality of city life soon set in. Finding stable jobs was harder than they anticipated, and making ends meet in a place like Chicago required more than just hard work. There were moments of doubt when it felt like the city presented more obstacles than opportunities.

Yet through it all, my parents kept pressing forward, never losing sight of why they had made the move in the first place. The struggles they faced in those early years shaped my understanding of resilience. Chicago, with all its complexities, became a backdrop for our growth. It was here that I learned to embrace change, adapt to the uncertainties of life, and see that growth often comes from stepping into the unknown.

I discovered that this move wasn't just about geography—it was about transformation. The challenges of starting over in a new place helped me see that each new horizon brings both opportunities and difficulties. It's through facing those difficulties head-on that we learn who we are and what we are capable of becoming.

Finding Strength in Adversity

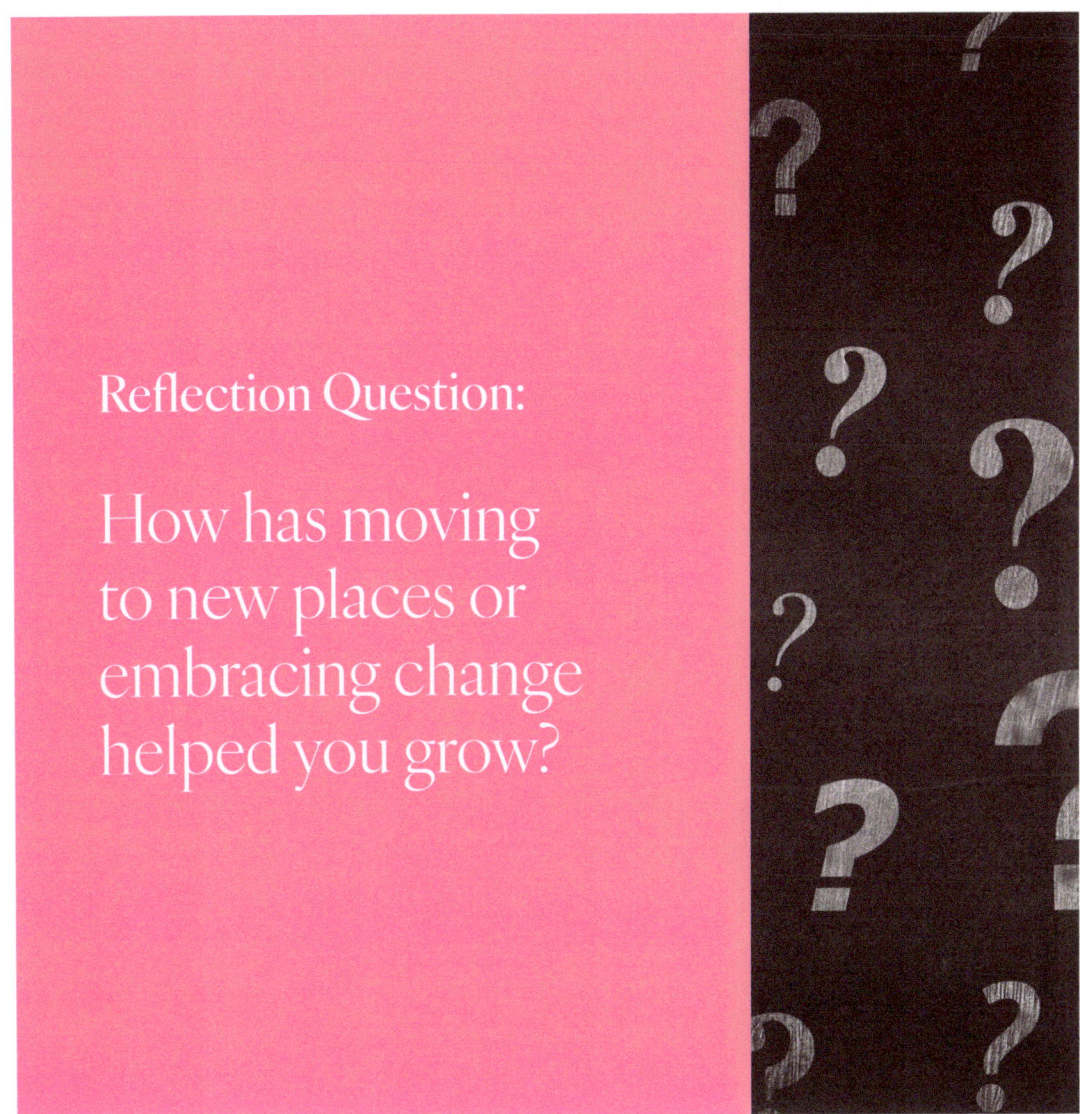

Reflection Question:

How has moving to new places or embracing change helped you grow?

Chapter 5:

Love and Challenges

Growing up, my father's battle with alcoholism cast a shadow over our family, creating challenges that we didn't always know how to face. It was hard for me to reconcile the man I loved with the person he became when alcohol took over.

My father was kind, loving, and always there for us when he was sober. He helped me with homework, played with us, and made me feel safe, but when he drank, he transformed into someone who was angry, distant, and unpredictable.

As a child, it was confusing to love someone so deeply and yet be afraid of the way alcohol changed them. I often found myself torn between my love for my father and the pain his addiction caused. It was difficult to see the person I adored fall into patterns of self-destruction. Yet, even in the darkest moments, I held on to the love that remained. That love didn't erase the hurt, but it gave me a way to navigate the complexities of our relationship.

Over time, I learned that loving someone through their struggles doesn't mean accepting their harmful behavior. It means finding compassion for their journey while also protecting your own well-being.

I had to create emotional boundaries, knowing that while I couldn't control my father's choices, I could choose how I responded to them. This taught me that love is not about perfect relationships—it's about seeing people in their entirety, even when it's difficult.

My father's battle wasn't easy to witness, but it showed me the importance of holding on to love, even when it's complicated. It taught me to seek understanding in difficult situations and to offer compassion to those fighting their own battles.

Finding Strength in Adversity

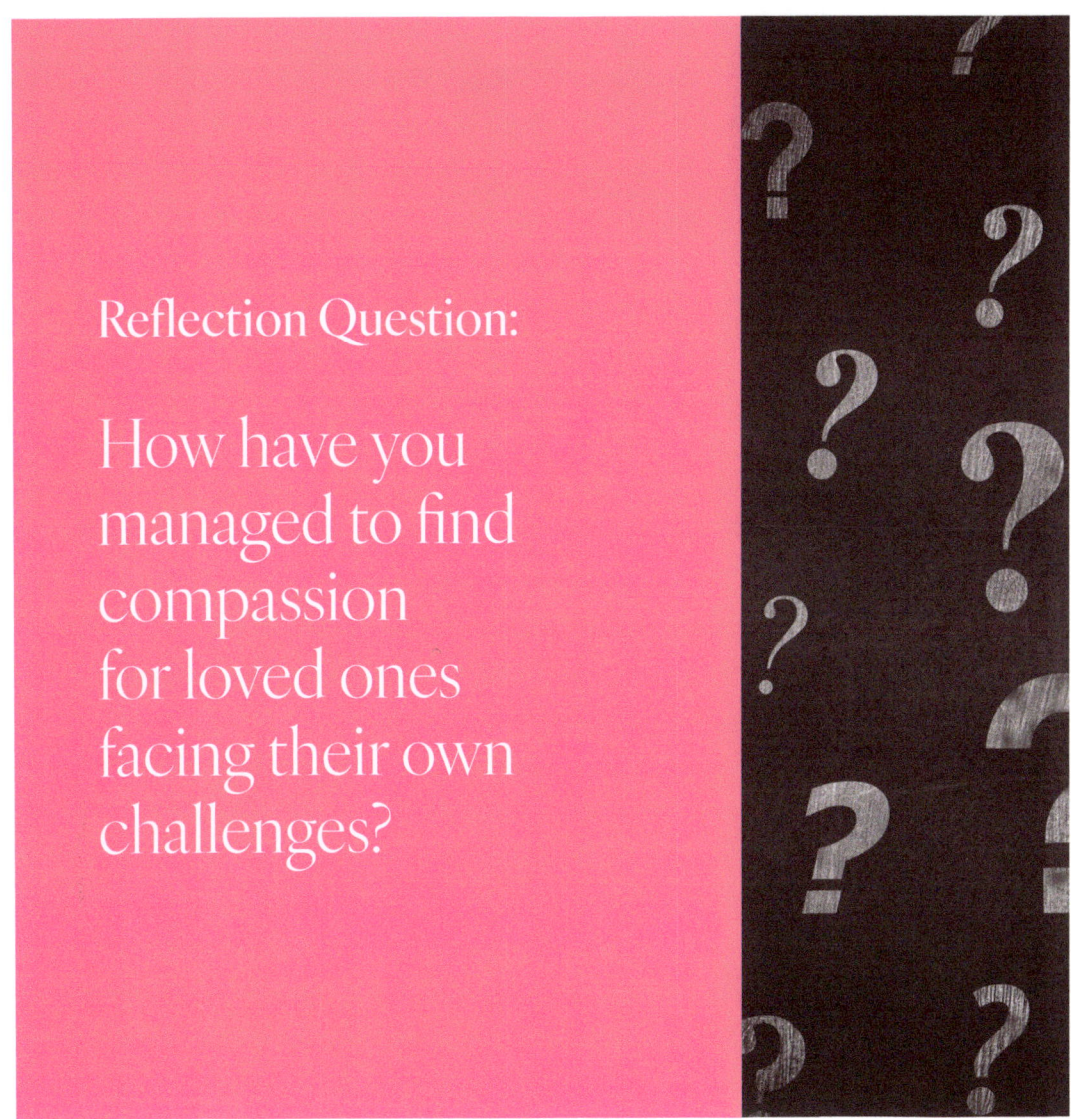

Reflection Question:

How have you managed to find compassion for loved ones facing their own challenges?

Chapter 6:

The Power of Community

Growing up, our family didn't have much, but we had each other and the strength of the community around us. In a way, our neighbors became our extended family. They were always there when we needed them, offering support in ways that seemed small at the time but meant everything to us.

I remember how one neighbor would watch us when my mother needed to work, and another would bring over meals when we couldn't afford much ourselves. These acts of kindness were more than just gestures—they were lifelines.

We didn't ask for help often, but it was always there, quietly offered without expectation. I began to realize that community isn't just about proximity. It's about shared humanity. In our hardest times, the people around us stepped in and filled the gaps that life had left. Their generosity and love provided a foundation of support that helped hold our family together.

As I think about those days, I am reminded of the powerful role community plays in all our lives. It's the quiet strength that helps us endure when things seem too heavy to bear alone. My neighbors' kindness showed me that we don't have to face life's challenges in isolation. Support often comes from unexpected places, and it can transform hardship into something manageable, even hopeful.

Looking back, I see that the power of community isn't just about giving—it's about the connection that arises when we allow ourselves to be vulnerable enough to receive help. That connection builds resilience, and in that shared experience, we find strength.

Finding Strength in Adversity

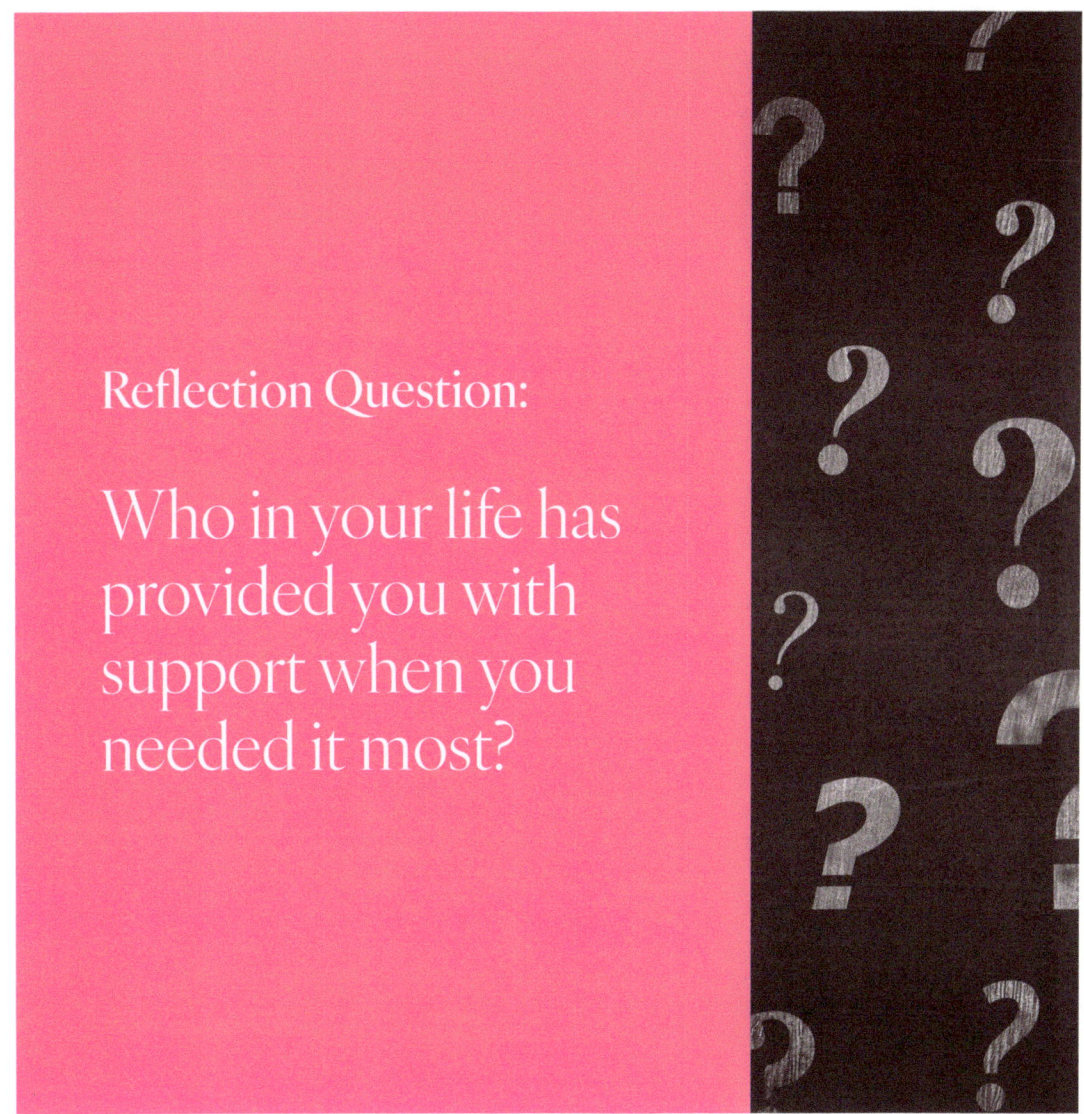

Reflection Question:

Who in your life has provided you with support when you needed it most?

Chapter 7:

Navigating Family Dynamics with Love

Growing up in a complicated household meant learning how to love through pain. My father's struggle with alcoholism was a constant source of conflict within our family. There were moments when I was confused and hurt by his behavior—torn between loving him and fearing what his addiction had done to him and us. It wasn't easy to understand why someone I adored could also cause so much pain.

As I grew older, though, I learned that love isn't about perfection. It's about seeing someone for who they truly are—flaws and all—and still choosing to care for them. My father was not defined by his addiction. He was still the man who cared for me, helped with my homework, and made me feel loved in countless small ways.

It took time, but I came to realize that loving him didn't mean accepting all of his actions. It meant setting boundaries to protect myself while still holding space for the love that existed between us.

Learning to navigate family dynamics was one of the most important lessons of my life. I discovered that even in the most difficult relationships, love and empathy could coexist with pain and disappointment. Balancing those emotions required forgiveness, not just of my father, but of myself as well. I had to forgive myself for feeling conflicted, for loving someone who wasn't always easy to love.

Through these experiences, I've learned that family isn't defined by perfect harmony but by the effort to love one another through difficult times. It's the willingness to show compassion even when it's hard and to acknowledge that love sometimes means creating boundaries that allow both people to heal.

Reflection Question:

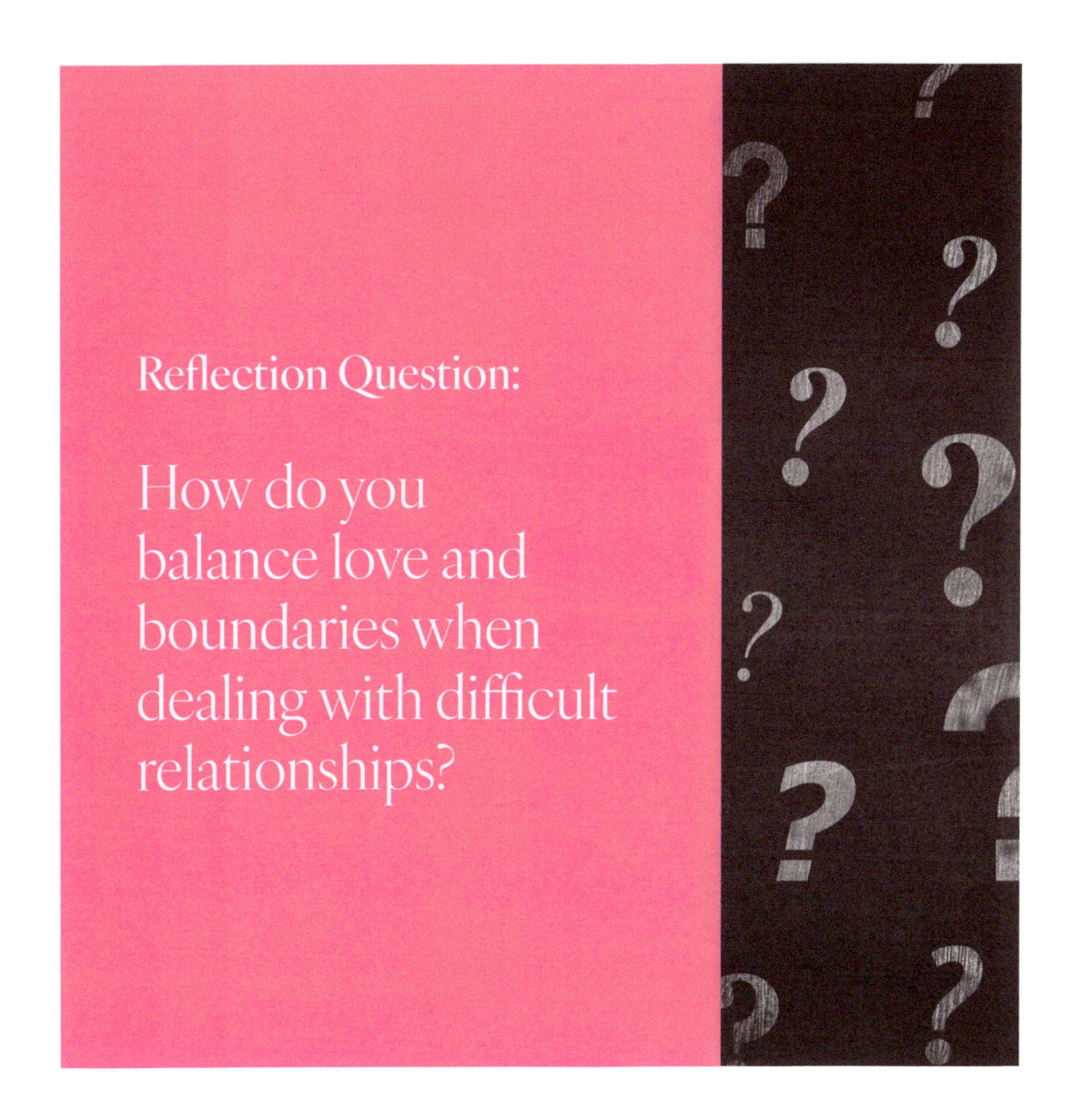

How do you balance love and boundaries when dealing with difficult relationships?

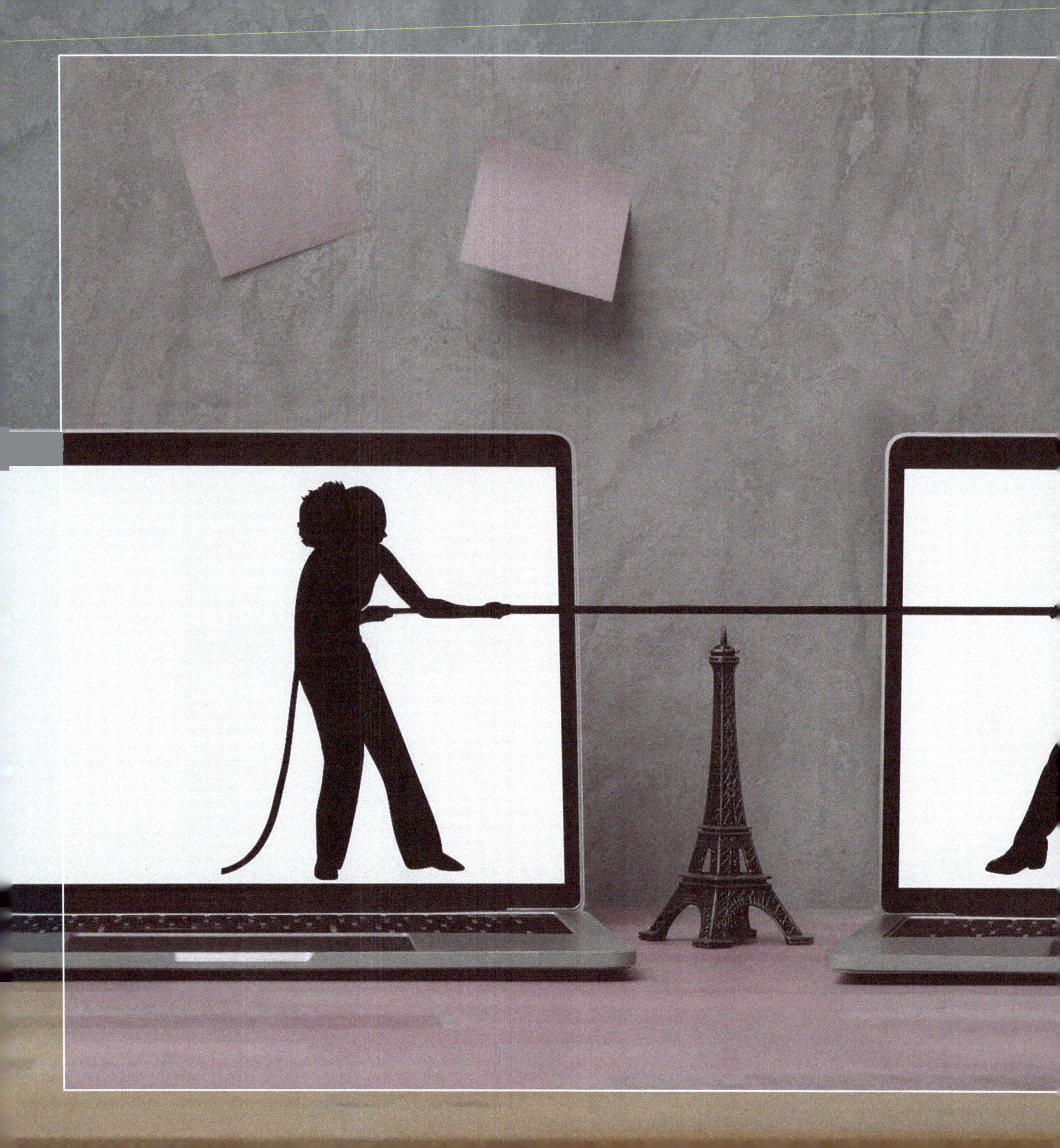

Chapter 8:

Choosing Love Over Conflict

The decision for my parents to separate wasn't just a painful moment in our family—it was a turning point. After years of trying to hold our family together, my mother made the difficult choice to leave my father. It wasn't because she stopped loving him, but because staying together was harming us all. Her decision wasn't about giving up; it was about choosing love in a different form—a love that prioritized our safety, well-being, and, ultimately, our healing.

At the time, I didn't fully understand why they couldn't make things work. I was close to my father, and watching him leave our home felt like the ground was shifting beneath me. However, as the years passed, I came to realize the strength it took for my mother to make that decision. She chose to protect us from the endless cycle of conflict, teaching me that love sometimes means making the hardest choices.

Choosing peace over conflict wasn't just an act of love for us—it was an act of love for herself, too. My mother's decision showed me that love doesn't always look like staying. Sometimes, it's about having the courage to walk away from a situation that no longer serves you, even when it's painful. Through her strength, I learned that protecting your peace and the well-being of those you love is a powerful form of love.

Looking back, I see that this decision, while heartbreaking, paved the way for healing. It taught me that real love isn't always about holding on—it's also about knowing when to let go for the sake of growth and harmony.

Reflection Question:

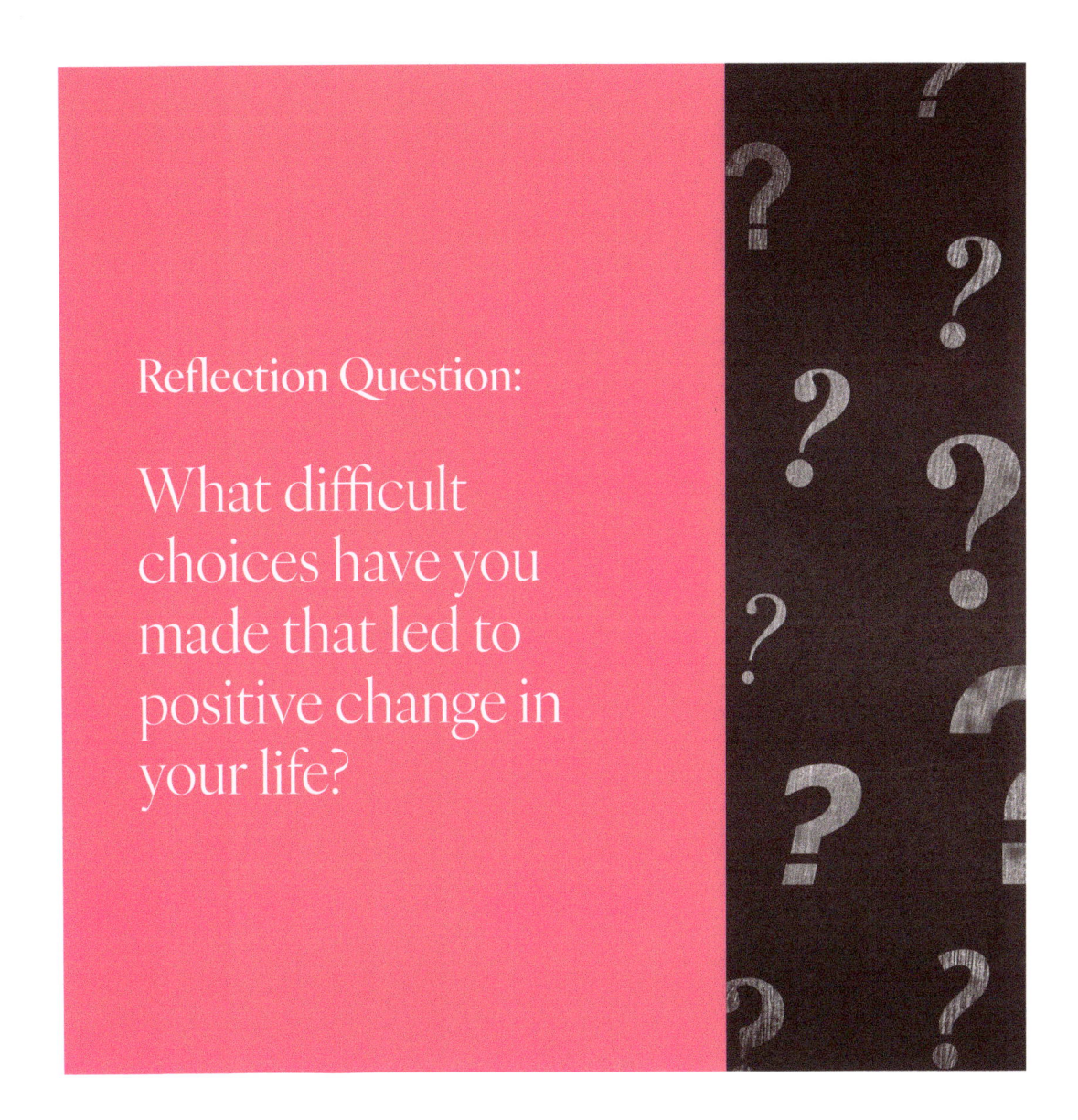

What difficult choices have you made that led to positive change in your life?

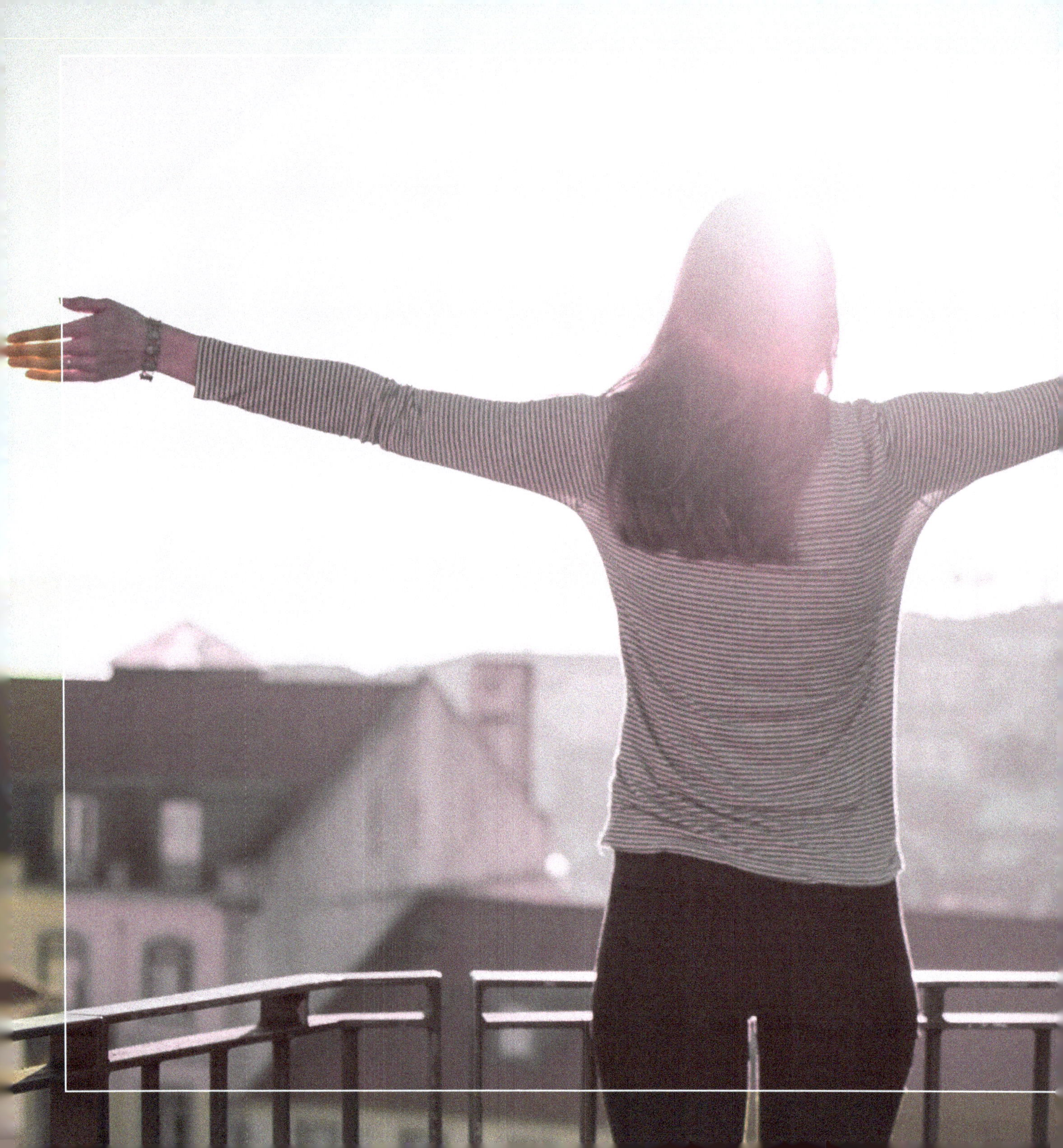

Chapter 9:

———

Learning from Life's Lessons

Life has a way of teaching us through both joy and hardship and for me, every challenge has held a lesson, even when I couldn't see it at the time. I used to wonder why certain things happened to me—why life seemed more difficult than it should be.

As I've grown, though, I've realized that the toughest moments were the ones that shaped me the most. I learned that strength isn't built in easy times. It's in the difficult moments where we discover what we're truly capable of.

There were moments of deep pain when I felt overwhelmed, like the weight of the world was pressing down on me, but with each experience, I became more resilient. I began to understand that hardships are not punishments—they are opportunities. Through them, I discovered inner strength, compassion for others, and a deeper understanding of myself. The challenges I faced gave me the tools to navigate life with more confidence, even when things didn't go as planned.

I've learned to reflect on each experience, both good and bad, and find the meaning within it. Whether it was a painful separation, a difficult move, or personal failure, each lesson has helped me grow into the person I am today. The most important thing I've learned is that life's hardest moments often lead to our greatest growth if we allow ourselves to embrace the lessons they offer.

Now, when faced with adversity, I remind myself that it's just another chapter in my story—a story of strength, resilience, and transformation. Life's lessons may not always come easy, but they are always worth learning.

Reflection Question:

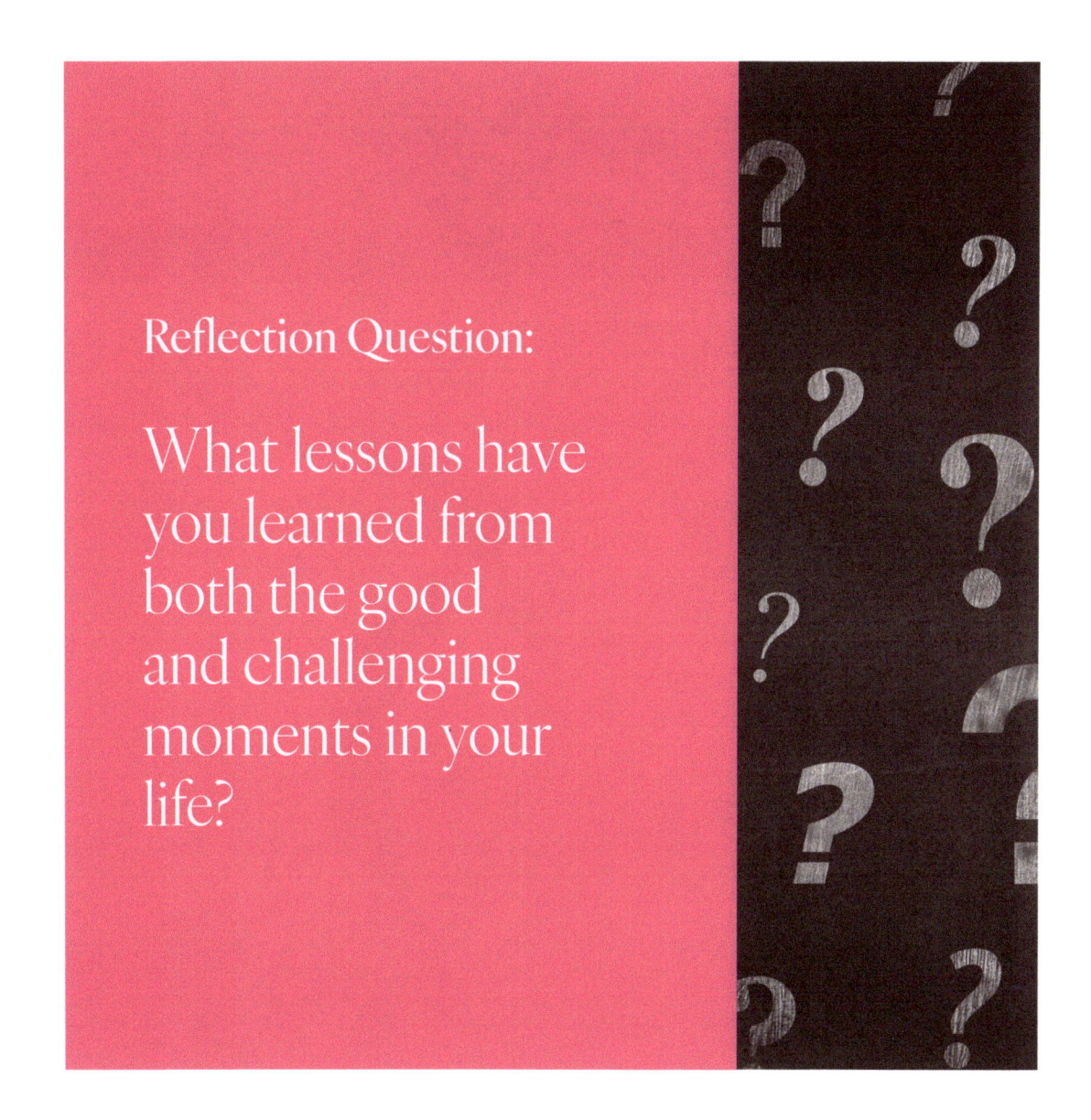

What lessons have you learned from both the good and challenging moments in your life?

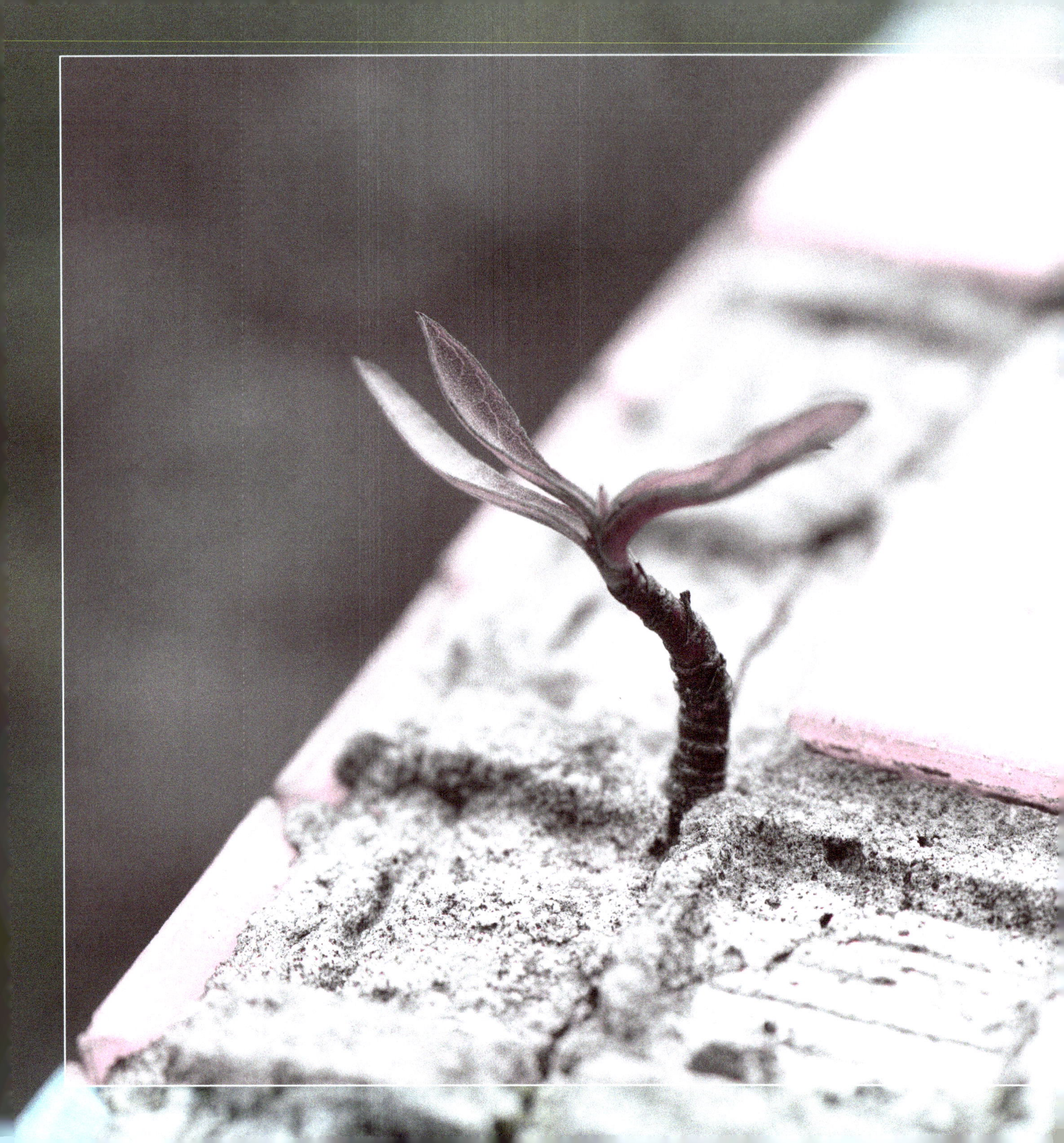

Chapter 10:

Embracing Hope in Adversity

No matter how overwhelming life became, I always tried to cling to hope, even when it felt like it was slipping away. In the darkest moments, hope wasn't just a feeling—it was a choice. I had to decide, again and again, to believe that better days were ahead, even when my circumstances made it hard to see.

Hope doesn't come naturally, especially when adversity seems endless. It's something I had to cultivate every day, like a seed that needed constant tending. I found hope in the small things—a kind word from a neighbor, a fleeting moment of peace, or the simple act of getting through another day.

These small sparks reminded me that no matter how bleak things appeared, there was still beauty in the world. Adversity didn't define me. How I responded to it did. In those times, hope became my compass, guiding me toward light even when the path seemed dark.

I've come to realize that hope isn't about ignoring the challenges we face but about finding the strength to face them head-on, with faith that something better is on the other side. It's about trusting that adversity will not last forever and that every chapter is part of a larger story. That trust gave me resilience—the ability to endure even the toughest trials—while knowing that I was growing through them.

In every hardship, I've discovered new parts of myself—strength, courage, and the belief that hope is the foundation of resilience. Hope isn't just the light at the end of the tunnel. It's what keeps us moving forward in the tunnel, step by step.

Reflection Question:

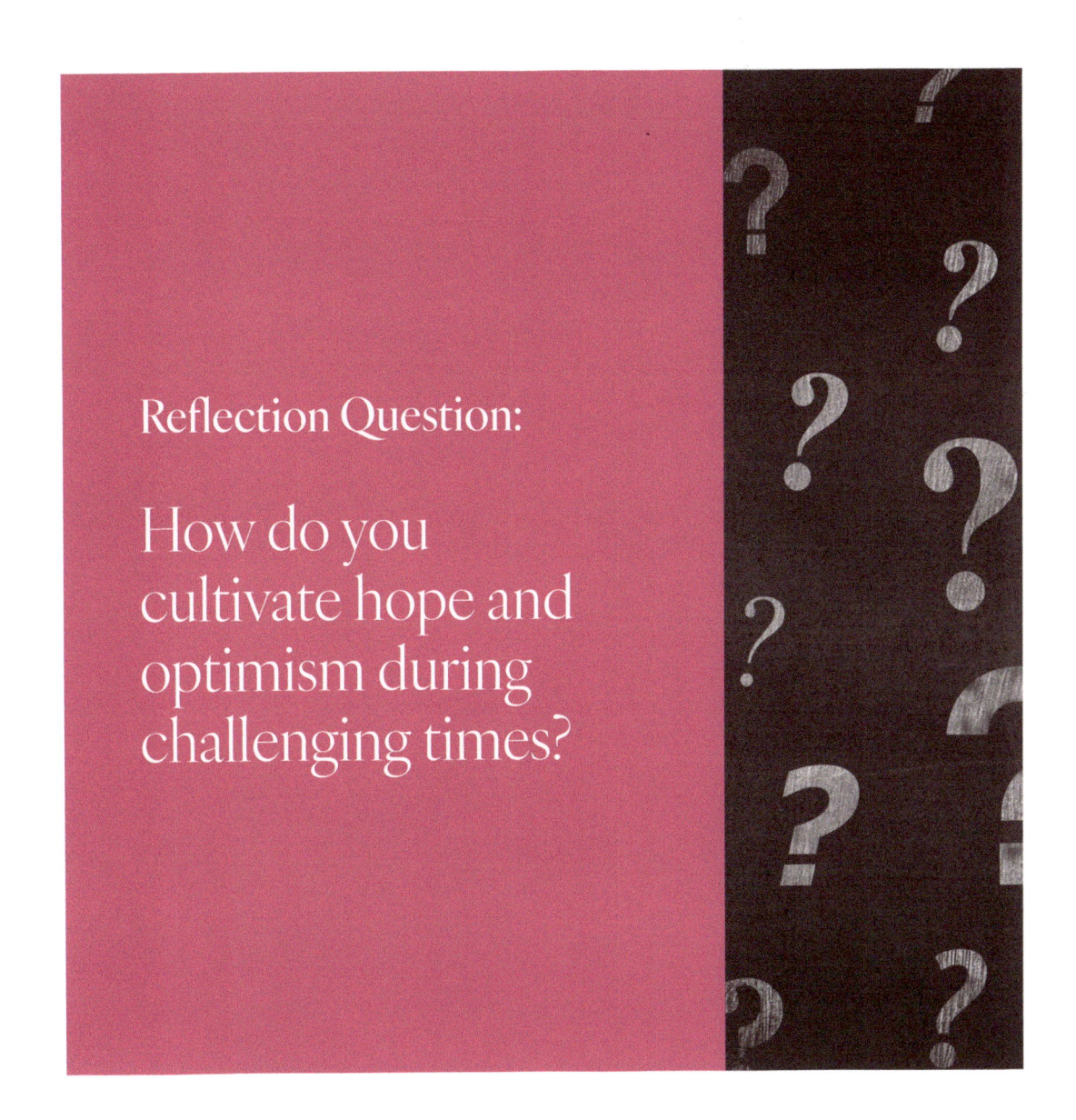

How do you cultivate hope and optimism during challenging times?

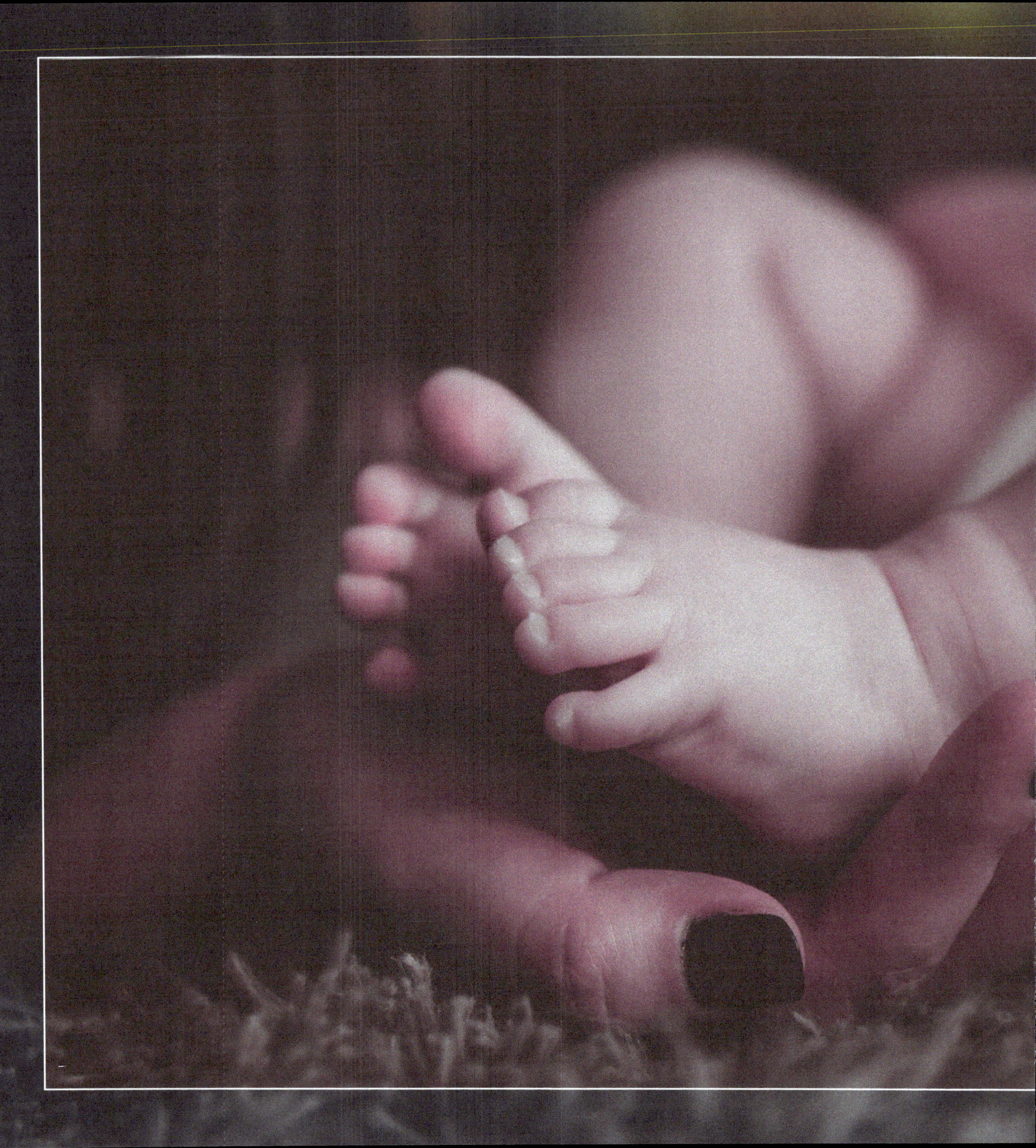

Chapter 11:

The Strength of a Mother's Love

My mother's love was like an anchor—steady and deeply rooted in everything she did. She was the heart of our family, holding us together through moments of chaos, pain, and uncertainty. No matter what challenges we faced, her strength never faltered.

It wasn't the kind of strength that was loud or obvious, but one that existed in the sacrifices she made every day to ensure we had what we needed. Her love wasn't just something we felt—it was something we saw in action each day.

There were many moments when I saw the weight she carried and the struggles she endured silently, all while keeping our home a place of warmth and safety. My mother worked tirelessly, often putting her own dreams and needs aside for our sake. She held our family together with her quiet confidence, and it was through watching her that I learned the true meaning of strength.

Her love was not just a comforting presence—it was a force that gave me the courage to face life's difficulties. She showed me that real strength isn't about never breaking; it's about getting back up each time you fall. Her love provided the foundation for my own strength, teaching me to rise above life's challenges with grace and perseverance.

I often reflect on the ways her sacrifices shaped me into the person I am today. Her example taught me that love and strength are intertwined and that the most powerful forms of both often go unseen. My mother's love was the quiet force behind every victory I've achieved, and it continues to guide me.

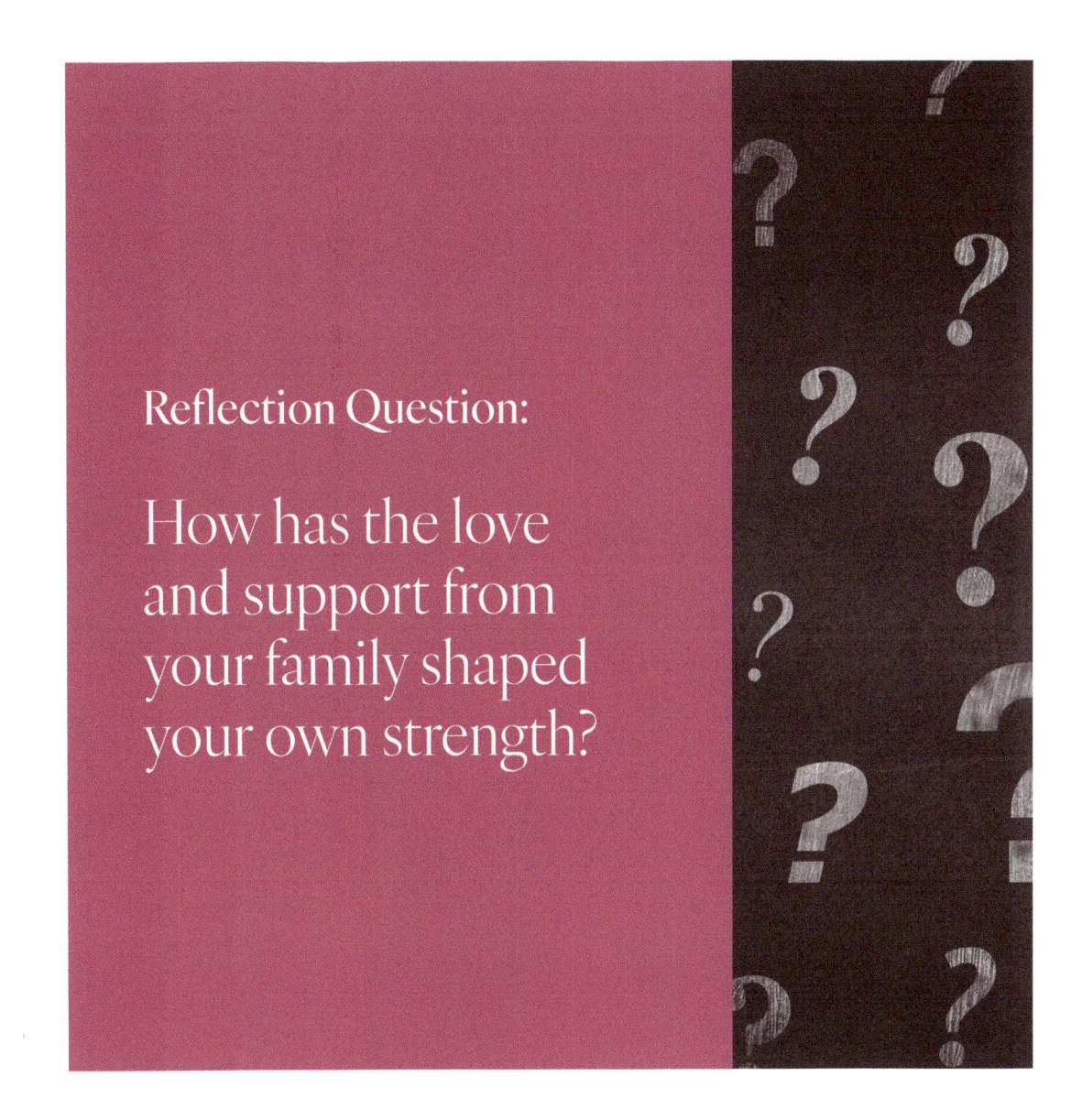

Reflection Question:

How has the love and support from your family shaped your own strength?

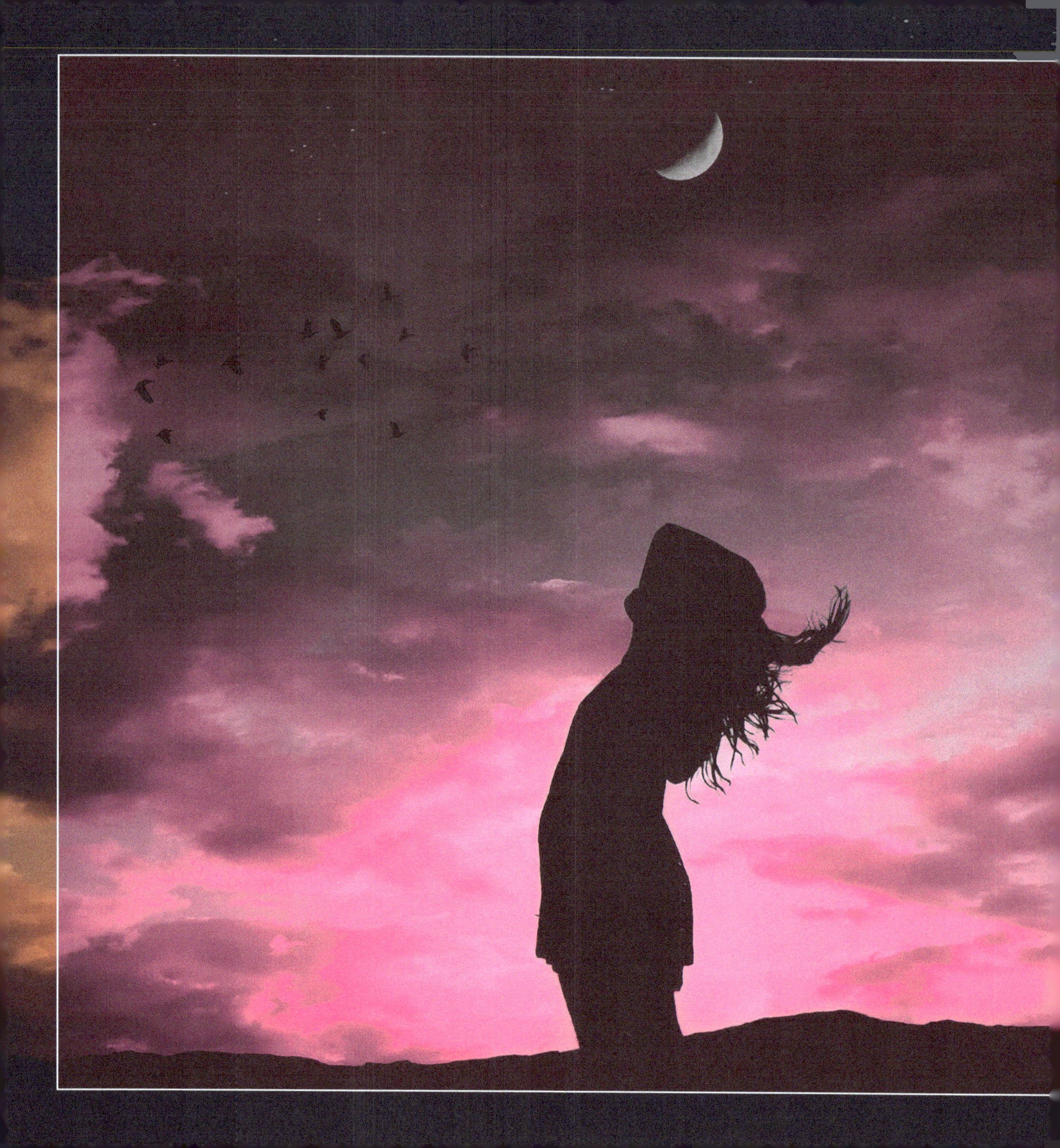

Chapter 12:

Finding Peace Through Reflection

There was a time when I couldn't find peace, no matter how hard I tried. I was constantly running—from pain, from the memories of hardship, and from the emotions I didn't know how to process, but as I've grown, I've learned that peace doesn't come from avoiding the past. It comes from facing it with courage.

Only when I allowed myself to sit with my experiences, both the beautiful and the painful, did I begin to find a deeper sense of calm and acceptance. Reflecting on my journey hasn't been easy. There were times when the memories felt overwhelming, with moments of heartbreak, loss, and confusion.

Yet, it was through this process of reflection that I began to understand my own resilience. By embracing both the light and dark parts of my journey, I have found peace in the balance. Every hardship taught me something, every joy reminded me what life could be, and through it all, I learned to see the whole picture rather than only the difficult parts.

Now, when I look back, I see not only the struggles but the growth that came from them. I realize that each challenge brought me closer to the person I am today, and with that understanding came a sense of fulfillment. For me, peace isn't about erasing the past but about accepting it and finding meaning in every step along the way.

Through reflection, I've discovered that peace isn't a destination but something to practice daily and requires honesty, vulnerability, and compassion for myself. In that practice, I've found the calm I once thought was out of reach.

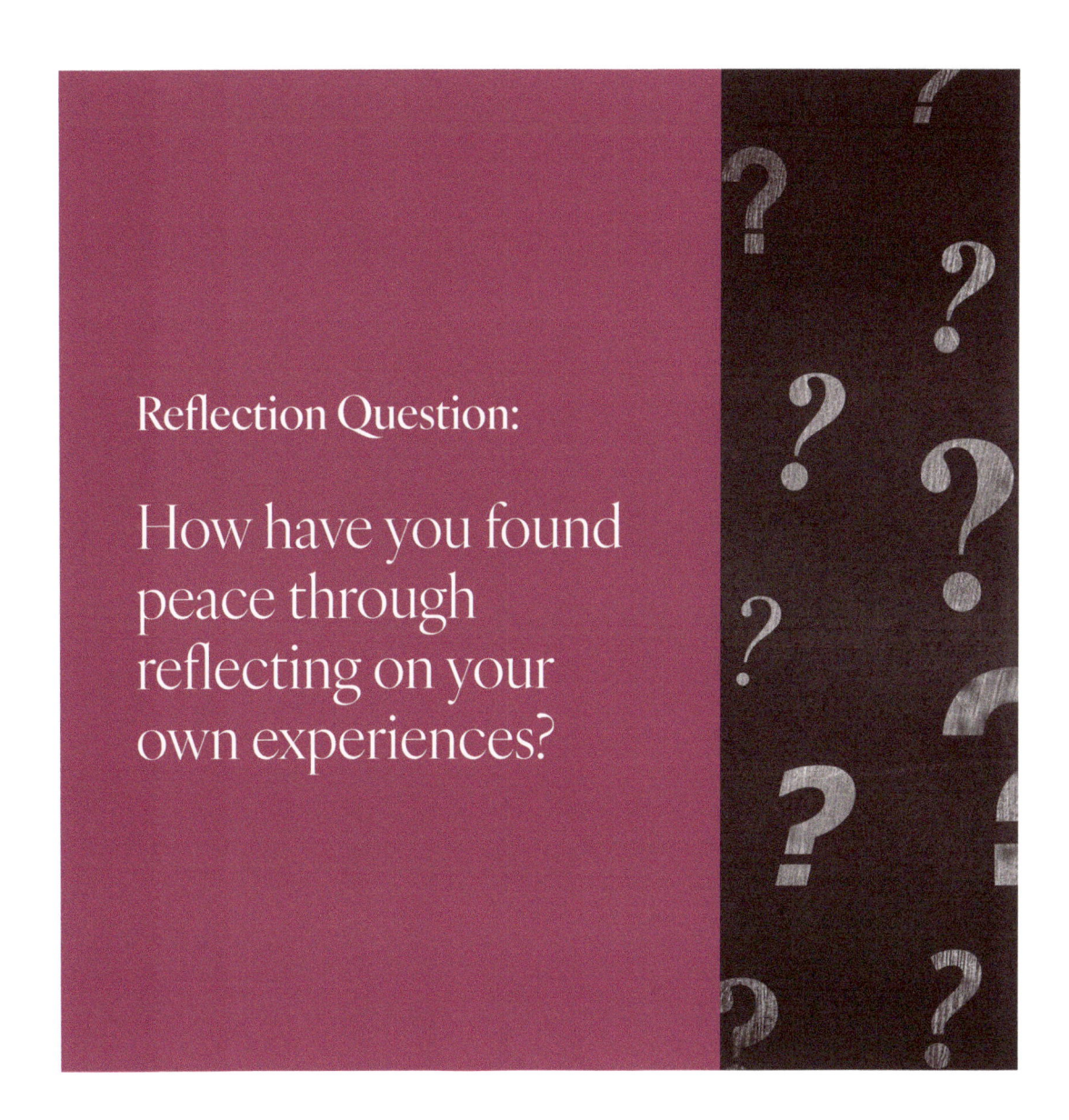

Reflection Question:

How have you found peace through reflecting on your own experiences?

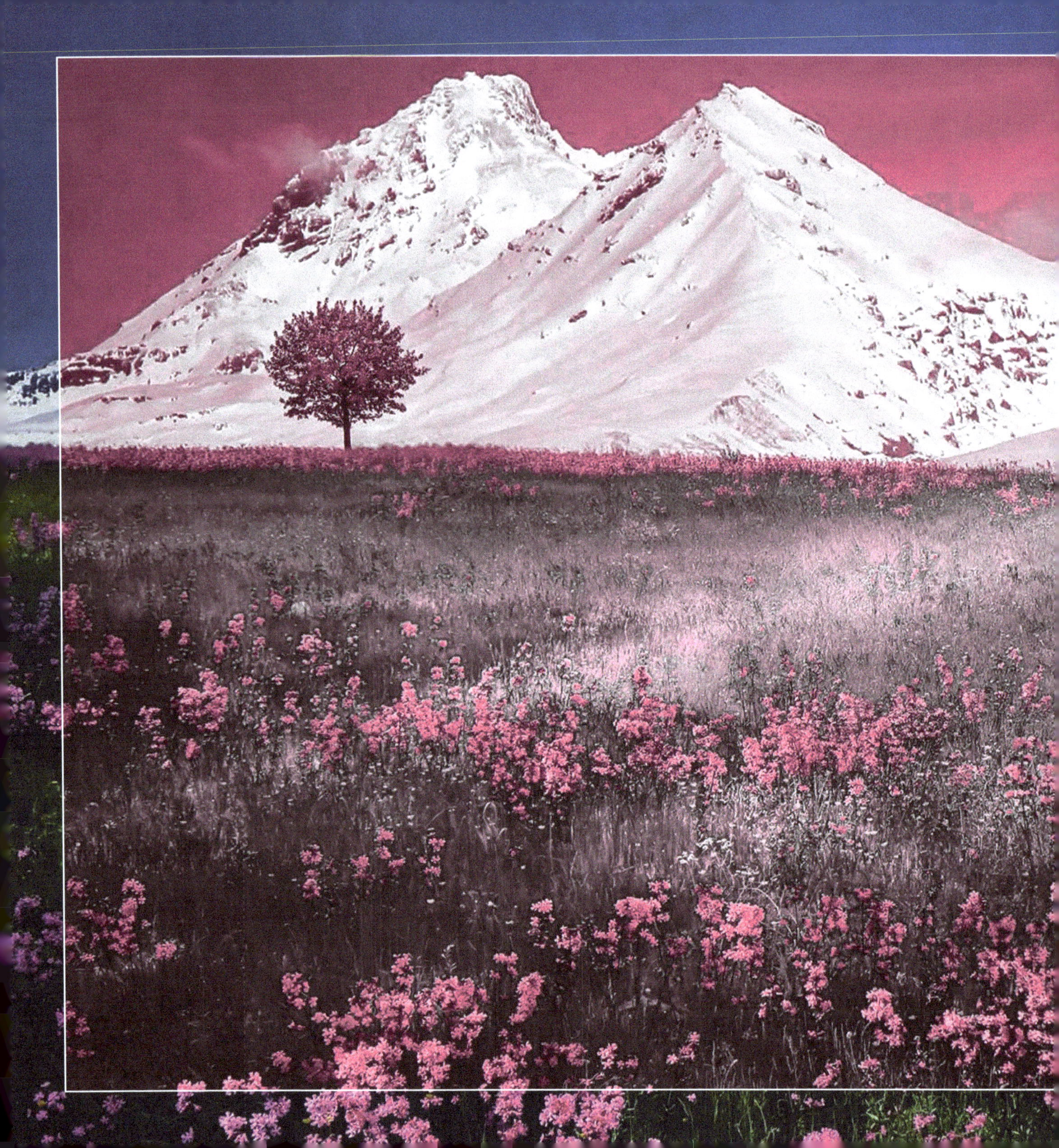

Chapter 13:

Inspiration and Hope for the Future

As I look toward the future, I carry with me all the lessons my past has taught me—the strength, resilience, and hope I found in moments of struggle. My journey hasn't always been easy, but I've learned that our experiences, both good and bad, shape us in ways we often don't realize at the time.

Each challenge I faced helped me discover my true self, and now, as I move forward, I do so with a heart full of gratitude and a spirit filled with optimism.

The future is bright, not because it's free from challenges, but because I now understand that I have the tools to navigate whatever comes my way. Every step I take is grounded in the belief that I can shape my life and turn every hardship into an opportunity for growth.

I've learned that life is not just about surviving the storms but about finding ways to dance in the rain. This has given me the courage to embrace the unknown and trust that the best is yet to come.

I want you to know that no matter what you've been through, you have the power to create the future you desire. Your past may shape you, but it doesn't define you. The resilience, hope, and strength you've built will guide you to the life you envision.

As you move forward, remember that every challenge is a stepping stone, every hardship is a chance to grow, and every dream you pursue is within reach. The future is filled with possibilities, and it's yours to create.

Reflection Question:

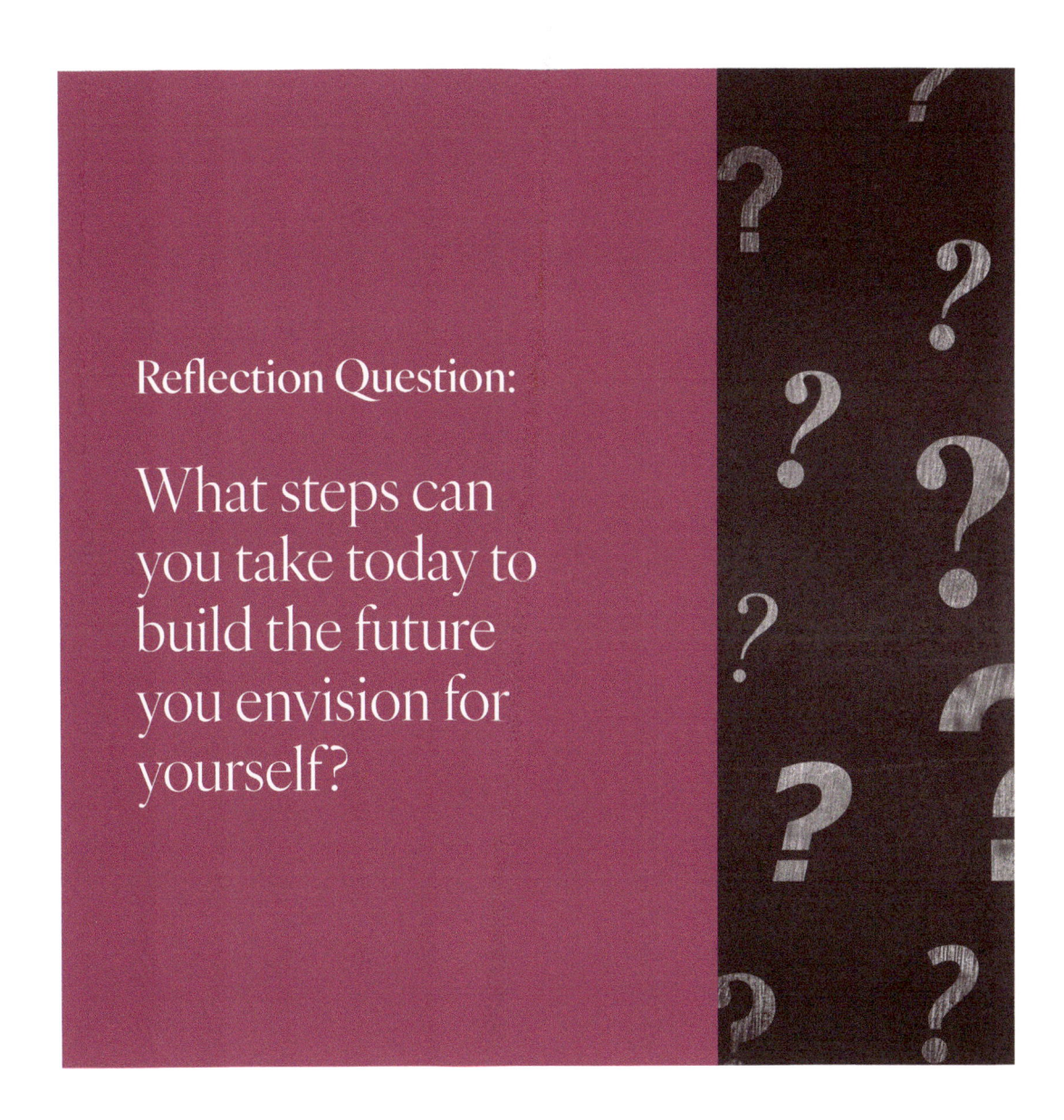

What steps can you take today to build the future you envision for yourself?

About the Author

Sheresse Winford is a determined woman who is living her newfound life helping and inspiring others in every way she can. She loves to travel, and she takes a solo trip every year to renew her spiritual strength.

Volunteering and being of service to the community is a very important part of Sheresse's life. She makes time for that when she isn't working at her full-time job in finance as a senior collection specialist and small business owner of Intouch Painting and Debris Removal.

Most importantly, Sheresse says, *"I love God with all my heart and soul."*